Weathering and Erosion

First published in 2005 by Evans Brothers Limited
2A Portman Mansions, Chiltern Street
London W1U 6NR

Consultant: Simon Ross, Editor: Sonya Newland, Designer: Big Blu Ltd.,
Picture Researcher: Julia Bird

Published in the United States by Smart Apple Media
2140 Howard Drive West, North Mankato, Minnesota 56003

Library of Congress Cataloging-in-Publication Data

Gifford, Clive.
Weathering and erosion / by Clive Gifford.
p. cm. — (Looking at landscapes)
Includes bibliographical references and index.
ISBN 1-58340-731-6
1. Weathering—Juvenile literature. 2. Erosion—Juvenile literature. I. Title. II. Series.

QE570.G54 2005
551.3'02—dc22   2005040506

9 8 7 6 5 4 3 2 1

Contents

Introduction

Earth is in constant change. Every day, all over the world, many different forces, processes, and cycles act upon it. As the land masses of continents slowly but powerfully drift apart or move closer together, rocks are forced upward to become mountains, or volcanoes erupt, creating new rock formations. While the landscape rises in some places, in others, it is gradually being worn down by other forces. This wearing away and lowering of the land surface is known as denudation. Weathering and erosion are responsible for denudation. They are caused by many different things, including water, wind, temperature changes, and chemical reactions. Sometimes, these agents can be powerful, such as when a giant glacier plows up the land and rocks that lie in its path, or when waves relentlessly pound a coastline. At other

▲ Floodplains such as this one in South Africa provide fertile farmland and were the places around which many ancient civilizations grew and thrived.

times, they can appear gentle, such as when chemicals in rainwater slowly dissolve rock, or when a desert wind forces small rock particles to rub against one another. Whether they are obvious to us or not, weathering and erosion have been responsible for shaping much of our planet's landscape.

Human activity has contributed to some processes of erosion; overgrazing, the diversion of valuable water sources for use in agriculture and industry, and the destruction of rain forests, which leaves the ground vulnerable to soil erosion, are just a few examples. But people have also used the processes of weathering and erosion for thousands of years. Some of the earliest civilizations grew up around the rich floodplains and deltas created by water erosion (see page 18).

From winding valleys, dramatic cliffs, and sweeping bays to structures such as the stone archways and enormous boulders scattered across desert regions, all have been created by the constant processes of weathering and erosion that have taken place over thousands of years.

▲ The results of erosion and weathering can be seen in many places. In Canada, these pits have been made in the rock by wind and water erosion.

▼ Some of the most dramatic features in landscapes all over the world have been formed by the processes of weathering and erosion. This pedestal rock stands in a desert valley in Utah.

Constant Cycles

Weathering and erosion are closely linked but are not the same thing. Weathering is the gradual breaking up and disintegration of rocks at or near Earth's surface. The process results in the weathered rock remaining in the same place. As soon as a loosened rock or rock particle begins to move away from its original site, the process of erosion has begun. Erosion involves movement and the removal of material from the landscape. Erosion can happen on its own, although it often occurs after weathering has taken place. Over time, the agents of erosion, such as rivers, seas, glaciers, and winds, create some of the world's most amazing landscape features.

▼ Horseshoe Bend is a spectacular example of the results of river erosion on rock over thousands of years. The Colorado River has cut a deep circular loop into the rocks on the border of Arizona and Utah.

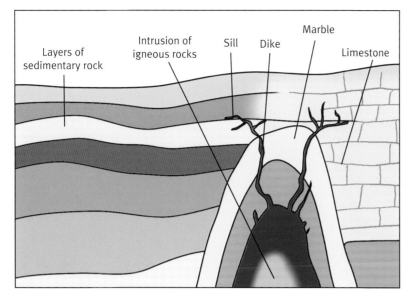

Layers of sedimentary rock | Intrusion of igneous rocks | Sill | Dike | Marble | Limestone

◀ Heat from hot igneous rocks, which have worked their way (intruded) into an area of limestone rock, turns the surrounding limestone into marble. Other igneous rock cools between layers of sedimentary rock, forming a sill. The igneous rock that has filled the cracks between rocks and turned solid is called a dike.

Rock types

Rocks are made up of chemical compounds known as minerals, and they come in many forms. Geologists (scientists who study rocks) classify all rocks into three basic types: igneous, metamorphic, and sedimentary.

Igneous rocks are formed from hot, molten rock, known as magma, that has cooled and hardened. The type of rock formed depends on the chemicals in the magma and how quickly it cools. When magma cools slowly, usually deep below Earth's surface, large crystals are formed, the rock has a coarse grain, and it is usually very tough. Granite is one of the most common rocks of this type. It has a whitish or gray flecked appearance and is very strong—granite can resist most types of weathering and is often used for buildings. When magma is close to or on Earth's surface, it usually cools more quickly. The rocks it creates—such as obsidian and basalt, the most common rock found on the ocean floor—contain much smaller crystals, which gives the rock a fine grain.

Metamorphosis means "change." Metamorphic rocks are so-called because they have changed from sedimentary, igneous, or other metamorphic rocks because of great heat or huge pressures. There are two main ways in which metamorphic rocks are created. In the first, igneous rocks spread in between other rocks. They are so hot that they "bake" the surrounding rocks. Marble is a metamorphic

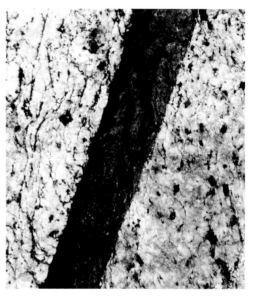

▲ Here, molten rock (magma) has intruded into a wall of granite (pink/gray). The igneous intrusion hardens to form different types of rocks.

Igneous rock types

Igneous rocks formed from magma that has cooled slowly deep beneath Earth's surface are called plutonic igneous rocks. Those that have cooled rapidly after erupting onto Earth's surface, or after rising up to fill cracks close to Earth's surface, are called volcanic igneous rocks.

▲ An ancient lava flow hardened to form the basalt columns of the Giant's Causeway, on the coast of Northern Ireland. Most of the 40,000 columns are six-sided, although some have four, five, or eight sides. The tallest of the columns are more than 39 feet (12 m) in height.

▶ Chalk is a type of sedimentary rock formed from the skeletons and shells of millions of tiny creatures. It is particularly common in north-western Europe and forms the famous white cliffs of the English coastline around Dover.

● Ores

Many useful minerals, such as the metals aluminum, copper, and iron, are found in rocks in chemical compounds called ores. Aluminum, for example, is found in the ore bauxite, 140 million tons (127 million t) of which is mined worldwide every year. An ore is impure (contains other substances), and after mining, the mineral has to be extracted using techniques developed by industry.

rock that has been changed from limestone in this way. Metamorphic rock can also be formed by the movement of Earth's crust, which causes rock to press together. Slate is formed from shale in this way.

Sedimentary rocks make up about three-quarters of the rocks on Earth's surface, and it is here that they begin forming. They are made up of tiny pieces of rock, minerals, or the decayed remains of plants and animals. Over time, these are pressed together by other materials deposited on top of them. Eventually, the original materials harden and form a rock such as limestone, sandstone, or mudstone. The process of erosion transports the sediments from which these rocks are formed.

What is the rock cycle?

Earth is a giant recycling machine. Water in rivers, lakes, seas, and oceans evaporates into the atmosphere, where it forms water vapor and clouds. It eventually falls back to Earth as rain, and the water cycle begins again. Rocks change in a similar way, but the rock cycle takes thousands of years.

In the basic rock cycle, igneous rock forms when molten magma cools and turns solid. Through weathering and erosion, particles of igneous rock are transported and deposited as layers of sediment that eventually form sedimentary rocks. Some of these rocks are transformed via heat and pressure into metamorphic rocks. Greater heat can result in metamorphic rock melting into magma, which forms new igneous rock.

The rock cycle is not always this simple, though. Igneous and sedimentary rock can both be heated to such high temperatures that they form magma. When this happens, new igneous rock is created. Weathering and erosion can affect all three types of rock, resulting in the formation of new sedimentary rock.

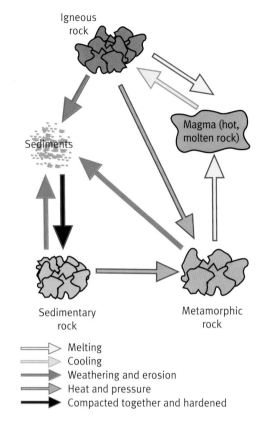

Igneous rock

Magma (hot, molten rock)

Sediments

Sedimentary rock

Metamorphic rock

⇨ Melting
⇨ Cooling
⇨ Weathering and erosion
⇨ Heat and pressure
➡ Compacted together and hardened

▲ The rock cycle is a way of charting the links between the changes that take place in the rocks on Earth. It also shows how weathering and erosion play important roles in the creation of new rocks.

● Fossils

Fossils are the remains, or the shape left behind by the remains, of prehistoric living things that have settled in sediment. Over many years, fossils are compacted and pressed into the sediment, and eventually, they become sedimentary rock. Fossils are a valuable tool for geologists—studying the types of fossils and the layers of Earth in which they appear can reveal much about prehistoric life on our planet.

▶ Coal is formed from the remains of prehistoric plants, which have been compressed into a solid material, similar to the way sedimentary rocks are formed. Coal is a valuable fossil fuel; more than 4.4 billion tons (4 billion t) of it are mined worldwide every year.

Causes and Effects of Weathering

▲ Over a long period of time, small pieces of rock, constantly buffeted by the moving waters of a river or the sea's waves, are turned into smooth pebbles.

Rocks are attacked and broken down by weathering, which takes place on or close to the surface of Earth. There are two main types of weathering—physical and chemical. Physical weathering occurs when rocks are broken into smaller fragments without any change in their chemical makeup. Chemical weathering occurs when a chemical change takes place in some or all of the minerals that make up the rock.

What causes physical weathering?

The main causes of physical weathering are sudden changes in temperature and extreme cold or heat. Changes in temperature can cause the "freeze-thaw action," which is when water collects in cracks in rocks during the day and then the nighttime temperature drops enough to make the water turn to ice. Most substances expand when they are heated and contract when cooled. However, when water freezes and becomes ice, it actually expands. The expanding ice increases the size of the cracks, forcing the rock apart and weakening its structure. Over a period of time, parts of the rock break away. The more often the temperature moves above and below freezing during the year, the quicker the rock is weathered away.

▶ During the freeze-thaw action, rain seeps into cracks in a rock. As the water freezes into ice, it expands, widening and lengthening the cracks. When the ice thaws, it allows more water into the rock. The cracks increase in size until parts of the rock break away.

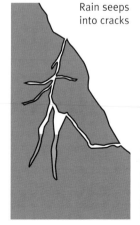
Rain seeps into cracks

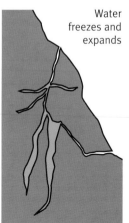
Water freezes and expands

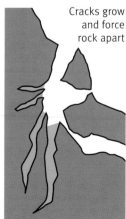
Cracks grow and force rock apart

Salt weathering is another type of physical weathering. It occurs mainly in hot deserts and on coasts. It relies not on freezing and thawing, but on water that contains high levels of salt. In this process, water enters cracks and pores—tiny holes in the rock—and heat causes the water to evaporate, leaving behind salt crystals. As more and more salt builds up, the crystals grow in size and cause parts of the rock to flake away or split completely.

▼ Physical weathering of this rock in England's Lake District caused piles of rock fragments called scree to form at the foot of the slope.

● Tafoni and exfoliation domes

In some desert areas and along coastlines, salt weathering can cause a honeycomb of pits and depressions in rock formations. These are called tafoni, a word that comes from the Mediterranean island of Sicily, where the coast is dotted with these patterns. Minerals expand when they are heated and contract when they cool. In desert areas, where the days can be very hot and the nights extremely cold, the expansion and contraction can cause the rocks to break apart. The outer layers of the rock are affected much more than the inner layers by the great temperature swings. As a result, the outer layers of rock eventually crumble or peel away like the layers of an onion, leaving rounded boulders or domes. This process is called exfoliation. Sugarloaf Mountain, which overlooks the Brazilian city of Rio de Janeiro, is a famous exfoliation dome.

▼ Sugarloaf Mountain in Brazil is an exfoliation dome, formed as swings in temperature cause the outer layers of rock to peel away, leaving the distinctive rounded shape of the mountain.

What causes chemical weathering?

Chemical weathering occurs when the minerals that make up a rock are chemically changed. There are several types of chemical weathering. In the process of oxidation, oxygen in the air reacts with iron in rocks to form iron oxide. This turns the outside layers of rock a rust red and also weakens its structure, making it crumble more easily and become more susceptible to other forms of weathering and erosion.

Most chemical weathering involves water. By itself, water causes weathering through a process called hydration, in which water is absorbed into the minerals in the rock, expanding and weakening them. Water can also react with some minerals found in rocks, such as feldspar, to turn rocks into clays in a process called hydrolysis. Other forms of chemical weathering occur when

● Uluru

Weathering of an area of land can create a large, isolated, rocky peak called an inselberg, the German word for "island mountain." Inselbergs usually occur in sandstone or granite. Geologists think they are the remains of a larger area of high land, most of which has been worn away by weathering and erosion.

The largest inselberg in the world is Uluru (formerly known as Ayres Rock), situated in the heart of Australia. It reaches a height of 1,141 feet (348 m), and its base is 5.8 miles (9.4 km) around. Uluru is a sacred site to the Aboriginal peoples of Australia and is a major tourist attraction.

▼ Uluru in Australia is an inselberg— a steep-sided hill made of solid rock.

Acid rain

Acid rain, caused by pollutants from industry and cars mixing with rainwater, can devastate forests and lakes. It can also severely damage rock, the surfaces of stone buildings, and statues. The acids formed in acid rain, usually nitric and sulfuric acid, dissolve limestone and sandstone, wearing them away.

▲ Chemical weathering in the form of acid rain has worn away the limestone stonework on York Minster, a cathedral in the British city of York.

substances dissolved in water react with the minerals in rock. When rainwater and carbon dioxide react, for example, carbonic acid is formed. When this comes into contact with certain rock types, such as limestone, it slowly dissolves the rock in a process called carbonation.

▶ The Valley of Fire in Nevada is largely made of sedimentary rock—a distinctive red sandstone. The layered effect shown here is the result of different rates of erosion of the various types of sedimentary rock.

What is biological weathering?

Biological weathering is caused by plants and animals and can result in either physical or chemical weathering. Some creatures, such as limpets, are capable of scraping away or burrowing into soft rock. They scrape a hollow out of certain rocks and embed themselves in it. When plants grow in the soil-filled cracks of rocks, their roots push on the sides of the cracks, widening them and eventually breaking the rocks apart. Large, strong tree roots can also grow along joints in rock, forcing an entire block to be detached.

● Limestone landscapes

Limestone is a common sedimentary rock formed from the shells and bony remains of microscopic creatures that have been compacted and hardened. Limestone usually forms in layers called bedding planes, which contain vertical cracks called joints. When rainwater combines with carbon dioxide in the air or from decaying plants and animals in the soil, a weak acid, carbonic acid, is produced. When this flows through cracks and joints in the rock and between bedding planes, it dissolves limestone and can form underground tunnels, caves, and other features of what is known as a karst landscape.

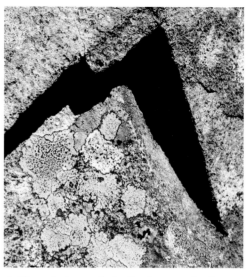

▲ When plants grow in the tiny fissures of rocks, they can cause the cracks to widen. Eventually, part of the rock will break away. This is physical weathering caused by biological processes.

▼ This limestone bedding plane (running diagonally through the center of the picture) was exposed by weathering of the cliff face.

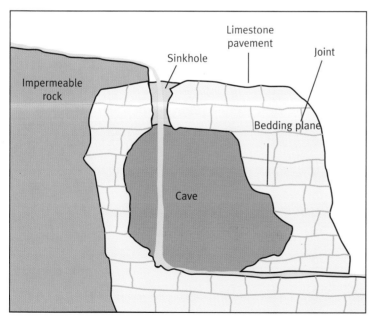

▲ A karst landscape is formed because of chemical reactions between water and air. Carbonic acid flows through joints in soil or the limestone pavement and wears away the rock, creating caves and tunnels.

Erosion by Moving Water

Erosion occurs when rock material is moved in some way. Water is the most powerful and widespread of all agents of erosion. Moving water in the form of seas, oceans, rivers, streams, and rainfall weathers and erodes landscapes all over the world. Water has the ability to erode wherever it is found. Even places that are now starved of water, such as hot, dry deserts, still have features created by water erosion in the long-distant past. In some desert regions, water once carved the rock to form flat-topped hills called mesas and smaller versions of mesas, known as buttes. Although water is usually rare in desert regions, some of these areas can be subject to sudden and extremely heavy rainstorms. These can erode and carve out steep-sided valleys called wadis.

▼ The extraordinary limestone peaks and pinnacles of the hills around Guilin, China, have been formed mainly through erosion by moving water. A high sea bed gradually eroded the limestone scenery, creating a deep gorge through which the Li River now flows.

How does rain cause erosion?

▲ These snow-covered buttes stand in Monument Valley, Arizona—a flat floodplain with several of these flat-topped hills.

Rainfall causes erosion in a number of ways. Rain-splash erosion happens when rainwater strikes the surface of the rock or soil. As the rain is absorbed by the land, it fills the tiny spaces between rock or soil particles and forces them apart. Over time, these particles are moved away from each other. Rain can also transport loose particles or materials that have already been weathered away from their original locations. Water erosion from rainfall works along with gravity to move material down slopes. When there is lots of rain, soil can become saturated—it can absorb no more water. As a result, more rain stays on the surface and becomes surface runoff. Because it is not absorbed into the soil, the water flows down slopes, carrying loose particles with it. In extreme cases, where there has been an unusually large amount of rain, the water can make the soil unstable, and it can crash down a slope with great force in the form of a mudslide.

La Guaira mudslide

In December 1999, the area around the Venezualan port of La Guaira experienced the equivalent of a year's rainfall in just two days. The heavy rains caused a giant mudslide, which swept away everything in its path, including rocks, trees, buildings, and people. An estimated 10,000 people died as a result of the disaster, and many thousands more were made homeless.

▶ Heavy rains in Venezuela caused mudslides that engulfed the town of La Guaira in December 1999.

▼ Abrasion is caused by large rocks or boulders, such as these in a river in Sweden. The debris is dragged along as the water flows, wearing away the riverbed and banks.

How do rivers cause erosion?

Rivers are natural channels that carry water downhill, sometimes for thousands of miles, before eventually joining up with lakes or seas. They normally begin high up in hills and mountains, where they are formed by rain or surface runoff. They can also be fed by underground water sources, known as groundwater, or by melted snow and ice. Rivers grow as they are joined by smaller rivers and streams, known as tributaries. As rivers travel along their courses to eventually empty into lakes, seas, and oceans, they can cause significant amounts of erosion.

There are four main ways in which rivers cause erosion:

- Abrasion
- Attrition
- Hydraulic action
- Corrosion

Abrasion is the main form of erosion in many rivers. It occurs when riverbeds and banks are bombarded with large pieces of debris, such as rocks or boulders that have been gathered along the river's course. These are dragged, bounced, and rolled along in the water; they crash against the rocks and soil in the riverbed and along the banks, loosening them and wearing them away. Sometimes this debris itself is eroded as pieces collide with each other and

the river bed, breaking into smaller fragments and becoming more rounded. This is called attrition.

Flowing water can be very powerful. As it rushes along its course, it can hit obstructions, including the sides of the river channel. This causes further erosion through hydraulic action. The water is forced into cracks in the rock, wearing it away. The pressure of the water in the cracks can also cause parts of the rock to break away.

Corrosion occurs when chemicals—usually dissolved in the water from rocks—attack softer rocks, such as limestone or chalk, gradually wearing them away.

A young river tends to move more quickly than one in its later stages. This speed can cut deep V-shaped valleys along the way. The river may wind around obstructions in its path, and this can form tongues of land called spurs, which jut out from the sides of the valley.

▲ River water may swirl rocks and pebbles around, wearing away the riverbed to form a deep, round hole known as a pothole. These potholes are in North Dakota.

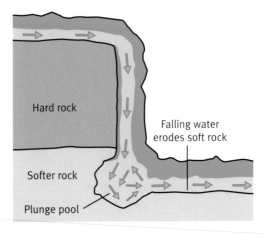

▲ A waterfall is created by erosion. Hard rock spans the riverbed; softer rock lying underneath is eroded by the water, creating a ledge. Undercutting of the softer rock may cause chunks of the harder rock to fall. Further erosion takes place where the water impacts, creating a plunge pool.

If a river quickly erodes downward while the sides remain steep, a gorge or canyon may form over a long period of time. When the river reaches its mature stage nearer sea level, the river channel is usually wider and shallower and often U-shaped.

Running water erodes different types of rock at different rates. Sometimes, a river erodes the base of its banks more quickly than rocks at a higher level. This means that eventually the base can no longer support the higher rocks and soil, and the bank will crumble into the water, widening the river. When rivers meet harder rock, which takes longer to erode, features such as rapids—where water flows very quickly around rocky outcrops—and waterfalls can form.

● The Grand Canyon

The Grand Canyon is one of the most spectacular sights on Earth. Situated in Arizona, the huge gorge stretches for 277 miles (446 km), with widths varying from 5 miles (8 km) to 18 miles (29 km). It was created over a period of 10 million years, mainly by the Colorado River eroding the surrounding rock. An array of mesas, buttes, and other dramatic rock formations can be seen throughout the canyon, and it is home to hundreds of species of birds, animals, and plants—several of them now endangered species. Rockfalls, mudslides, and wind erosion contribute to the canyon's great size, which is slowly increasing. More than 441,000 tons (400,000 t) of sediment are estimated to be removed from the canyon by erosion every day.

▶ This satellite image shows the Grand Canyon, formed over the last 10 million years by erosion caused by the Colorado River (flowing from top right to center left).

Niagara Falls

The magnificent Niagara Falls is situated on the Canada-United States border. This series of massive waterfalls is visited every year by millions of awestruck tourists watching the estimated 1.5 million gallons (5.5 million l) of water that flow over the falls every second. Since the formation of the falls more than 12,000 years ago, erosion has caused them to move backward a distance of approximately 7 miles (11 km). Today, the Canadian Falls section retreats about five feet (1.5 m) every year.

▶ Niagara Falls lies on the border between Canada and the United States. There are two main falls—these are the Canadian Horseshoe Falls, the larger of the two, which carry about 90 percent of all the water that flows through Niagara Falls.

Where does all the eroded material go?

The rate of erosion caused by a river depends on the speed with which it moves. The faster the water travels, the more powerful it is at carving and grinding away at the surrounding landscape. As a river matures, it usually crosses flatter land. It slows down and starts to deposit the eroded material collected by its waters. The larger debris is deposited first, and then the muds, silts, and sands are gradually left behind as sediment.

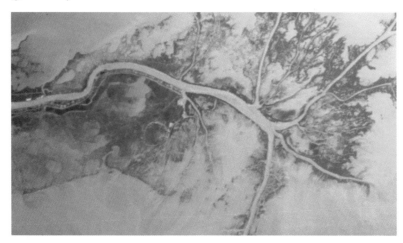

◀ The powerful Mississippi River empties around 10.6 billion cubic feet (300 million cu m) of sediment into the Gulf of Mexico every year. As this satellite photograph shows, the sediment has formed a giant delta in the shape of a bird's foot, covering more than 30,000 square miles (77,000 sq km)—more than twice the size of Belgium.

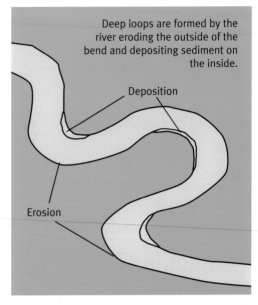

Deep loops are formed by the river eroding the outside of the bend and depositing sediment on the inside.

Deposition

Erosion

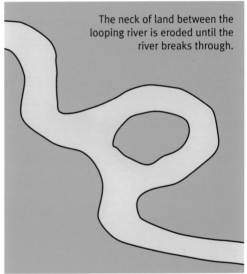

The neck of land between the looping river is eroded until the river breaks through.

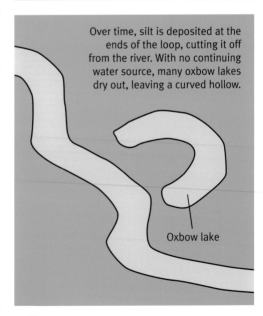

Over time, silt is deposited at the ends of the loop, cutting it off from the river. With no continuing water source, many oxbow lakes dry out, leaving a curved hollow.

Oxbow lake

A mature river rarely runs in a straight line. Instead, it bends and curves through the land; this is called meandering. When a river flows in a bend or loop, its current is faster on the outside of the loop than on the inside. The faster-flowing current continues to erode land, while sediment is deposited on the inside edge. Meandering can cause small beaches to appear on the inside of bends and can form oxbow lakes. As a river enters a lake or sea, it slows down and drops much of its remaining sediment. Large rivers carry huge amounts of sediment. Sometimes, more of this is dropped than the tides or currents can carry away. When this happens, layers of sediment build up and form an area of flat land called a delta. Many deltas are fan or triangle shaped. The gradual rise in sediments can eventually cause the river to break up into smaller channels to carry the water to the sea.

● Floodplains

When a river floods, it covers the land on either side of its banks with water containing sand and mud. The heaviest sediment is dropped first, and this stays closest to the river, forming low walls or banks called levees. Farther away from the river, lighter silts and mud are deposited; these remain even after the water moves back. Over many years of repeated floods, layers of extremely fertile land build up. These are floodplains, and they have been vital to the development of human life. Many of the world's pioneering civilizations built farming settlements on floodplains close to rivers such as the Nile in Egypt, the Indus and Ganges in India, and China's Huang He.

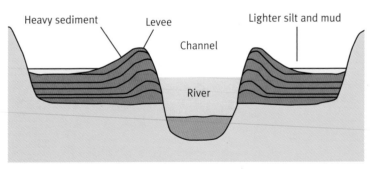

▲ Floodplains are created when a river floods its banks and then recedes. Shallow banks called levees are formed around the river channel by the heavier material. Lighter silts and muds are carried farther away.

The sea and coastal erosion

Powerful and relentless, the tides and waves of seas and oceans bombard the rocks, cliffs, and shores of Earth's coastlines. Like riverbanks, coastlines erode in a variety of ways. Hydraulic action (see page 21) can be a particularly erosive force, when strong waves force air into the cracks of a cliff face. The rocks, pebbles, and sediment that waves carry and hurl against the land act as a powerful abrasive. This debris not only attacks the coastline, but is also rounded and worn down to form smooth pebbles, sand, and more sediment. Seawater is slightly acidic and can dissolve limestone and chalk rocks, for example, attacking the weaker parts of cliffs and eventually causing them to collapse.

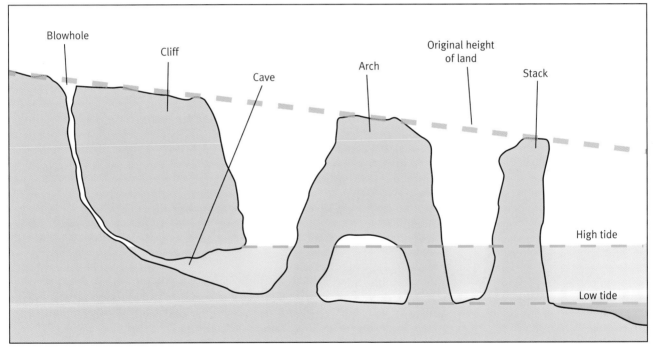

Many coastlines are formed from a mixture of hard and soft rocks, which erode at different rates. Sea caves are created by waves attacking areas of softer rock in coastal cliffs. The cave may begin as a very narrow crack that waves can penetrate. The waves exert tremendous force, cracking the rock from within. Sand and rock carried by waves produce additional erosive power on the cave's walls. A vertical hole, called a blowhole, which stretches from a cave to the top of a cliff, can form when water erodes vertical joints in the rock. Water and sea spray can be forced up and out of the blowhole by the power of the waves.

▲ Coastal erosion causes many familiar features. Caves are formed in parts of cliffs that are made of softer rock. Arches are formed from harder rock, which is eroded much more slowly. When the roof of an arch is eroded away completely, stacks are left.

▶ Durdle Door, on the coast of Dorset in southern England, is an example of an arch. Over thousands of years, the soft limestone of the headland has been worn away by erosion.

▼ The Twelve Apostles is an unusual series of rock stacks on the southern coast of the Australian state of Victoria. The stacks are remnants of rock left behind as erosion by the sea wore away the surrounding cliffs.

Softer rock can be worn away into curved bays. Harder rock is left behind to form cliffs and headlands, which stick out into the sea. Back-to-back caves can form at the base of a headland, and over a long period of time, this can form an arch. Further erosion collapses the roof of the arch, leaving a formation called a stack. Beaches are formed from some of the loose sediment and stone created by coastal erosion and from material deposited by rivers as they flow into the sea.

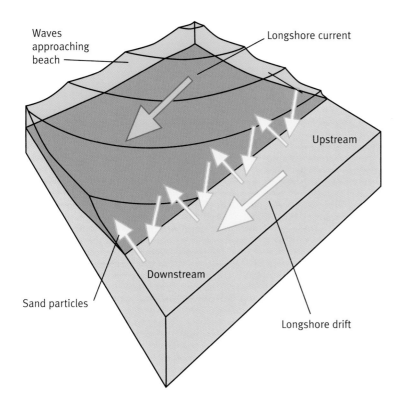

Waves approaching beach

Longshore current

Upstream

Downstream

Sand particles

Longshore drift

Longshore drift

Longshore drift occurs when waves move toward the coast at an angle. The waves moving up the beach (the wake) carry material up and along it. The waves retreating down the beach and back into the sea (the backwash) carry material back down the beach at right angles. This process slowly moves material sideways along the shoreline. Breaks in the coastline can result in longshore drift pushing beach material into the sea to form long, thin ridges called spits.

◀ Longshore drift occurs when material carried in the sea is moved up and along the coastline by the power of the waves traveling up and back at an angle.

◀ Spurn Head in Humberside has been formed by the deposition of sand across the estuary, carried by longshore drift.

Holderness

Coastal erosion occurs in many parts of the world. Holderness, on the northeast coast of England, has one of Europe's fastest-eroding coastlines. The land—which stretches for a distance of about 47 miles (75 km)—is being eroded at an average rate of 6.5 feet (2 m) every year, threatening coastal communities and agriculture. Part of the reason for the rapid erosion there is that the cliffs are made from material left behind when a glacier retreated, which is very susceptible to erosion. The constant wearing away of the cliffs at this location has a long history. Fifty villages in the region that were mentioned in the 1086 Domesday Book have disappeared completely.

Erosion by Ice

We have already seen how ice can weather rocks by repeatedly forming and thawing in the cracks. Glaciers—large masses of ice that move very slowly—are even more influential in shaping landscapes. Glaciers frequently form in mountain valleys, where there is heavy and regular snowfall. This snowfall is packed down by layers and layers of snow. As this happens, air is pushed out, and the particles of snow are pressed closer together. Eventually, large masses of solid glacier ice are formed, and gravity pulls them gradually down the valley like a slow-moving river. As long as more snow gathers at the source of the glacier than melts away at its front, the glacier will continue to creep downward.

Most glaciers advance very slowly—between one-third of an inch (1 cm) and three feet (1 m) a day—but they do so with incredible, irresistible force. Little can stop a glacier on the move. Rocks in a glacier's path can be plowed aside or plucked from the surface as the glacier moves, eroding the rock underneath and to the sides. At the base of the glacier, huge pressure creates heat, which melts the ice to form a film of water called meltwater. Picked-up rocks refreeze in the glacier's base and grind away at the land surface.

▶▲ The Devil's Postpile (right), 200 miles (320 km) east of San Francisco, is formed of basalt pillars. A glacier later ground its way over the Devil's Postpile, eroding the rocks and giving the formation a distinctive flat top (above).

Greenland's galloping glacier

Glaciers usually advance at a very slow rate, but occasionally a glacier will undergo a sudden surge, which can cause it to move at up to 100 times its normal speed. This phenomenon is known as galloping glaciers. In 1999, two scientists noticed a particularly fast-moving glacier in Greenland. They had studied the glacier four years previously and, on returning, were surprised to see how far it had moved. When they monitored it using satellite data, they realized that it was traveling at speeds of up to 100 feet (30 m) per day. The reasons for this are uncertain, but the speed may have been caused by meltwater from a mountain ice cap, which can seep underneath a glacier and act as a lubricant, carrying it along. It has also been suggested that changes in temperature and pressure made the glacier stick to the rock; when this happened, vast amounts of ice built up behind it and eventually forced it to break free and move forward swiftly.

▼ There are several examples of galloping glaciers in Greenland, possibly caused by water melting from a mountain ice cap and moving underneath the glacier, carrying it along.

Fjords

Fjords are another product of glaciation. They are long, deep, and narrow inlets from the ocean, bounded by steep-sided cliffs. The west coast of Norway is inundated with fjords, but they also occur elsewhere, particularly along the coasts of British Columbia in Canada, Alaska, New Zealand, Iceland, and southern Argentina. The largest fjord in the world is Admiralty Inlet, on the northwest coast of Baffin Island in Canada; it is 20 miles (32 km) wide at its mouth, narrowing along its length of about 230 miles (370 km).

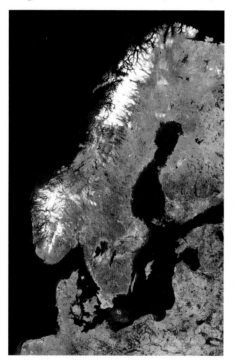

▲ The Scandinavian coast has many deep inlets called fjords; the peninsula was formed by the movement of glaciers during the last ice age.

What landscape features do glaciers leave behind?

Today, one-tenth of all land on Earth is covered by glaciers, which hold about 75 percent of the world's freshwater. Most of this takes the form of the enormous ice sheets that cover most of Greenland and Antarctica, and the 100,000 mountain glaciers around the world. During Earth's ice ages, even more land was covered in glaciers. The effects of glaciers' erosive powers on the landscape can be seen in many parts of the world. The formations left behind in highland areas can often be dramatic, with sharp ridges, bowl-shaped cirques, and jagged peaks. Mountain valleys that were once V-shaped have often eroded into a wide and deep U shape. In lowland areas, much of the vast amount of debris gathered and carried by glaciers is deposited as glacial drift. This is made up of boulders, gravel, sand, and clays, and often becomes fertile farming land. Glaciers leave behind anything they pick up along the way, which can include huge rocks. These are called erratic boulders and often look out of place in their landscape—which is not surprising, as the glaciers have moved them far away from their source.

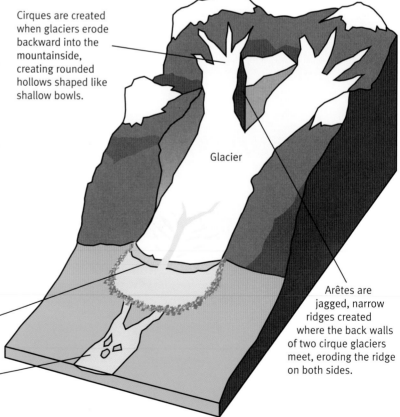

Cirques are created when glaciers erode backward into the mountainside, creating rounded hollows shaped like shallow bowls.

Glacier

The snout is the front face of a glacier. Rock debris can form a ridge, called a moraine, ahead of the front of the glacier.

Drumlins are long, teardrop-shaped sedimentary formations.

Arêtes are jagged, narrow ridges created where the back walls of two cirque glaciers meet, eroding the ridge on both sides.

▼ The 14,685-foot-high (4,476 m) Matterhorn mountain in Switzerland was created by several glaciers eroding a mountain top until all that remains today is a dramatic, steep-sided, pointed peak with sharp ridges.

Erosion by Wind

Like water and ice, wind has the power to erode landscapes by wearing away rock formations and moving large quantities of small rock particles such as sand and dust, leading to the formation of sand dunes beside lakes and along shorelines. Wind erosion can also cause large dust storms, which deposit quantities of fine material across the landscape, as well as being one of the major causes of soil erosion. But wind erosion has the greatest effect in desert landscapes and in other areas where there is little moisture.

▲ A sandstorm sweeps through the Kalahari Desert in southwest Africa; desert winds like this can reach speeds of 62 miles (100 km) per hour, and the swirling sand particles can have an erosive effect on land features.

Wind has a number of different erosive effects on landscapes. Because it can carry and move large quantities of small rock particles, it can be very erosive—especially as desert winds can reach speeds of 62 miles (100 km) per hour. Hard grains of rock particles carried by wind have a powerful, sandblasting effect on the solid objects they hit. Motor vehicles used in desert areas, for example, lose their paint in just a few years. This abrasive effect acts on rock, polishing it and cutting grooves through softer rocks in a formation. When different rocks are layered on top of each other, the softer rocks are eroded more dramatically than the tougher material. This can lead to undercutting and the creation of a rock pedestal—a large rock mass supported by only a thin neck or base (see page 7).

▶ One of the arches found in Arches National Park in Utah. The holes in the rocks of these natural bridges were originally formed by water erosion, but are believed to have been shaped and enlarged by wind erosion. The hole in the largest, Sipapu's Rock, is now more than 265 feet (81 m) across.

▲ Ventifacts are rocks that have been eroded and shaped by the wind. This ventifact was found in Bull Pass in Antarctica.

● Ventifacts and yardangs

Abrasion caused by wind erosion results in a number of distinctive features in deserts, including ventifacts and yardangs. Ventifacts are pebbles and rocks that have been shaped, polished, and sometimes rounded by many years of wind abrasion. Yardangs are streamlined hills that usually run in the direction of the wind. Yardangs are found in many of the hot, dry deserts in the world, including the Gobi Desert in Mongolia and the Mojave Desert in the U.S. Large yardangs, sometimes called mega-yardangs, are a major feature of Iran's Lut Desert.

Shifting sands and dust

When we think of deserts, we usually think of stretches of sand, but in fact, nearly half of Earth's desert surfaces are made up of stones and rocks. Winds blow sands and other loose particles away from an area, and over a long period of time, this can lower the surface level of the land. This process is called deflation. Deflation often leaves an exposed desert pavement strewn with rocks, pebbles, or gravel. In the Sahara Desert, rocky pavements stretch for distances of more than 620 miles (1,000 km). Deflation can also create hollows in the desert landscape. In places where underground water reaches the surface of these hollows, salt lakes or an oasis may form.

Winds carry finer, lighter dust particles high into the atmosphere. Winds greater than approximately 12 miles (20 km) per hour can force sand grains—heavier than dust—to hop and bounce along. As they land, they hit other grains, resulting in more movement. This process is called saltation. The sand grains can hit other rock particles that are too heavy to fly into the air, but which can be pushed along. This is called surface creep, and it accounts for nearly a quarter of all movement in a desert. Much of this moving matter forms seas of sandy hills known as dunes. If the wind blows regularly in one direction, these dunes can migrate, or move, up to 100 feet (30 m) in a single year.

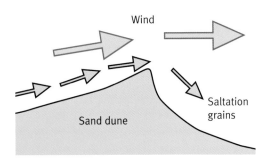

▲ A massive dust storm over the Sahara Desert (across the center of the picture). The U.S. Global Change Research Information Office estimates that winds move between 66 and 217 million tons (60-200 million t) of dust from the world's largest desert, the Sahara, each year.

Wind

Saltation grains

Sand dune

▲ Saltation, or surface creep, causes sand to move up a gentle slope of a dune and over its highest point, or crest, creating a steeper slope on the far side.

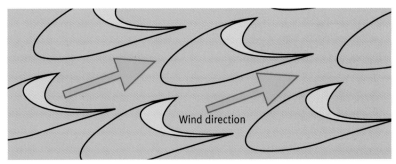

Wind direction

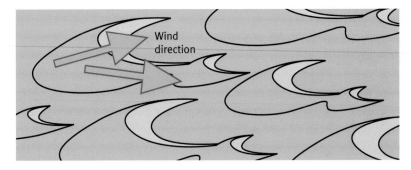

Wind direction

▶ When the wind blows constantly in one direction, crescent-shaped dunes, called barchan dunes, may form. If the wind direction shifts or winds blow regularly from two different directions, a seif dune may form.

● The Sossuvlei dunes

The Namib Desert in the African nation of Namibia is home to the Sossuvlei dunes, believed to be the world's highest sand dunes. Originally washed to shore by ocean currents, winds have shifted the sand farther and farther inland, causing the dunes to grow in size. The largest dunes in the Sossuvlei area rise more than 985 feet (300 m).

▼ Different types of sand dunes occur depending on the wind direction and obstructions in the way. The dunes in the Sossuvlei region of the Namib Desert are the highest in the world. The ripples in the foreground are also caused by wind erosion, forming at right angles to the direction of the wind.

Living with Weathering and Erosion

Weathering and erosion usually take place over long periods of time. Their effects may not appear as instant and dramatic as an earthquake, a flood, or a volcanic eruption, but they have major impacts on the development of human civilization, and they continue to affect the daily lives of millions of people.

Human activity itself has also had an effect on the erosion process. Humans are capable of causing weathering and erosion in a number of ways—from the impact of thousands of pairs of feet tramping across rock or land in a renowned tourist area to large-scale activities such as mining and construction. Intensive farming and the clearing of huge parts of the world's forests have contributed to the most serious form of erosion threatening millions of people today—soil erosion. For

▼ These level areas of land cut into the side of a steep hill in Malaysia are called terraces. Terracing can help combat soil erosion by retaining water in the ground and making it harder for soil to be washed or blown away down the slope of the hill.

Shelterbelts of new trees are being planted in an effort to halt the process of soil erosion in areas where trees have been destroyed and the soil damaged.

example, many of the world's rain forests are being destroyed. This not only causes problems for the animal and plant life that exists there, but also accelerates the erosion process. Once the trees have been cut down, the rich soil is exposed and is quickly washed away by rain, making it difficult for anything new to grow. Trees and grass provide a protective layer against erosion; when they are removed to make way for tourist buildings or for agricultural purposes, this protection is lost. All of the nutrients are washed away, and no new soil can form.

Topsoil is the fertile upper layer of soil crucial to farming. Natural processes take around 500 years to create an inch (2.5 cm) of topsoil, but topsoil can be eroded by wind or water in only a fraction of that time. Many different events can lead to soil erosion, but one of the most significant is the removal of vegetation, such as the clearing of trees or grass for farms or the overgrazing of animals. Without plant roots to bind the topsoil, and without plants themselves providing cover, the topsoil is exposed and can be more easily blown or washed away. When this occurs repeatedly, the land's ability to support life and farming decreases. At its most severe, large-scale soil erosion around the edges of the world's deserts can lead to desert growth. Up to 23,000 square miles (60,000 sq km) of new desert are created every year.

China's Sorrow

Massive soil erosion in the Huang He basin in China has caused great damage to farmlands and put the lives of thousands of people at risk. Heavy summer rains and a lack of plant cover resulted in an astonishing 1.5 billion tons (1.4 billion t) of sediment being washed from the land into the Huang He river (also known as "China's Sorrow"). Much of this sediment was transported into the ocean, but some settled on the river bed, raising its height. When the river banks are breached, flooding can cause massive loss of life. In 1939, more than a million people died in the region.

▲ The Huang He river in China has been subject to severe soil erosion, causing flooding and great loss of life.

The Aral Sea

The Aral Sea in Uzbekistan was once the fourth-largest inland sea in the world. It had plentiful fish and a busy marine trade. However, in the 1960s, human activity caused the flow of water into the sea to drop dramatically. Agricultural projects, such as irrigation put in to channel the water to help grow crops upstream, used up much of the water that once flowed into the sea. Today, the sea level is 46 feet (14 m) less than it once was, and more than 60 percent of its volume has been lost.

▲ A fishing boat beached in the Aral Sea—much of which is now a sandbank.

How can we use the effects of weathering and erosion?

People have used the results of weathering and erosion for many thousands of years. The first permanent shelters used by humans were caves formed from the wearing away of limestone and other rock formations. The good, fertile soil created by the vast quantities of sediment deposited in floodplains and deltas attracted some of the world's earliest settlers and farmers.

▼ Dredging lakes prevents them from silting up.

Many other examples exist of how people have turned the products of weathering and erosion to their advantage, from using weathered materials such as sands and clays in building to leisure pursuits such as skiing, hiking, and caving, which may rely on landforms created by these processes. The valleys, landforms, and waters left behind by glaciation have been exploited by people for hundreds of years. In the Rhone Valley in Switzerland, for example, farmers have long channeled meltwater from the glaciers above their farmland to irrigate their fields. In many countries, hydroelectric power (HEP) stations situated in valleys carved by running water or ice rely on the flowing river water to generate electricity without pollution.

All over the world, weathering and erosion have created fascinating and often spectacular features that attract large numbers of tourists. More than four million people visit the

Dust storms and loess

Winds can whisk away large amounts of dust and fine rock particles and carry them long distances. Dust from the Sahara Desert in Africa, for instance, often travels with the wind and falls in rains over Europe. When this dust is finally deposited on the ground, it is known as loess. Over time, it can build up highly fertile lands. Fine particles created by glaciers during the Ice Age have created thick layers of loess in the U.S., across Europe, and in many other countries. In China and other parts of Asia, the layers of loess deposits are more than 660 feet (200 m) thick.

Grand Canyon every year. Almost four times that number make trips to Niagara Falls. Wide, smooth beaches formed through coastal erosion in countries with a warm, sunny climate attract many more millions of vacationers. These people stimulate local tourism, which is one of the largest sources of income in many countries and regions.

The Dust Bowl

In the 1930s, severe droughts in the southern Great Plains, coupled with high winds, created an occurrence that became known as the Dust Bowl. Due to the overgrazing of cattle and a lack of rain, many plants died. With few roots to hold the soil in place, winds blew much of the fertile top layer away from the region. Thousands of farming families were forced to leave the area, which finally recovered in the 1940s.

▲ A farmer and his son flee an oncoming dust storm during the Dust Bowl of the 1930s.

◀ This hydroelectric power station is located in China. Water is a renewable energy source and does not pollute the environment.

What problems do weathering and erosion cause?

Weathering and erosion pose a wide variety of problems and challenges. Chemical weathering, for example, can cause major damage to historic buildings built of limestone; spreading root systems of trees can uproot cement. Weathering and erosion cause rockslides and rockfalls, which can injure people and obstruct roads. Erosion can undercut river banks, making them crumble. Sediment deposited in river mouths can clog the channels and may need to be repeatedly dredged to keep the channels clear for shipping.

The benefits and problems of erosion and weathering are sometimes interlinked. For example, while the erosion of the northeastern coast of England (see page 27) is a major problem, much of the sediment is deposited on the coastlines of Belgium, Germany, and the Netherlands, where it helps to form a natural sea defense against coastal erosion. There are also problems in fighting coastal erosion, which threatens clifftop or beachside communities. Various sea defenses, such as sea walls and wooden groynes jutting out into the sea, have been built to try to slow or halt coastal erosion, but coastal management is incredibly complex. In many instances, these defenses prevent erosion in one area but can cause it in another.

▲ A house balances precariously on the edge of a cliff eroded by waves and salt in Norfolk, England.

● Cape Hatteras lighthouse

Built in 1870, the 223-foot-high (68 m) Cape Hatteras lighthouse is the tallest lighthouse in the U.S. In a little over a century, coastal erosion removed about 1,310 feet (400 m) of land between the lighthouse and the ocean, threatening its survival. In 1999, after almost 10 years of campaigning and planning, an expensive engineering project resulted in the 4,960-ton (4,500 t) lighthouse being moved 2,890 feet (880 m) to protect it from the threat of further coastal erosion.

▼ Sea walls such as this one in Madeira are put in place to reduce the effects of water erosion on coastlines.

Problems caused by landslides

Erosion of material on mountains and hillsides can sometimes become a major problem. The sudden collapse or downhill movement of a large mass on a hillside is called a landslide. Landslides can be caused by a number of events, including earthquakes and volcanic eruptions, but many are the result of exceptionally high levels of rainfall, or snow and ice melt. The over-steepening of slopes through human activity, such as building and mining, can also cause landslides. Landslides are a serious threat to human settlements. In the U.S., for example, it is estimated that they cause up to $2 billion in damage and kill between 25 and 50 people every year.

● Disastrous landslides

In 1980, a massive landslide down the slopes of the Indian tea-growing region of Darjeeling, triggered by heavy rains, killed more than 250 people. A year later, in the Sichuan Province of China, heavy rains caused a massive landslide that took the lives of 240 people and rendered 100,000 homeless. In 2003, a landslide engulfed much of the mining town of Chima in Bolivia, causing death, injury, and the loss of 400 homes.

◀ Landslides, like this one in Switzerland, triggered by erosion and weathering, can cause great damage and loss of life.

Glossary

abrasion The physical wearing and grinding of a surface through friction and impact by material carried in air, water, or ice.

acid rain Rain and snow containing harmful chemicals, caused by burning fossil fuels.

arête A jagged, narrow ridge created where the back walls of two cirque glaciers meet, eroding the ridge on both sides.

attrition When pieces of river debris collide with each other, eroding into even smaller fragments.

bay An area of the sea enclosed by a curved section of the coast.

bedding plane A layer in a limestone rock formation containing vertical cracks called joints.

biological weathering Weathering caused by plants and animals living in the cracks in rocks.

butte A small, flat-topped hill or plateau, similar to a mesa.

canyon A deep, narrow valley with high, steep sides.

carbonation The process by which rainwater and carbon dioxide react to form carbonic acid, which dissolves certain types of rock.

chemical weathering When the chemical composition of rock changes.

cirque A bowl-shaped depression on a mountain that is carved out by a glacier.

corrosion When chemicals dissolved in water from rocks attack softer rocks such as limestone, wearing them away.

crust The outermost part of Earth.

deflation The removal of clay and dust from dry lands by strong winds.

delta The often triangular-shaped alluvial deposition area at the mouth of a river.

denudation The lowering and wearing away of a land surface through weathering and erosion.

desert A hot, dry region with little or no vegetation.

dike Igneous rock that has seeped between layers of sedimentary rock and hardened.

dissolve To make a solid substance or a gas disappear into a liquid.

drumlin A long, teardrop-shaped sedimentary formation.

dune A hill or mound of sand formed by wind erosion.

erosion The movement or removal of material from a landscape.

evaporation The process by which a liquid, such as water, is changed into a gas when it is heated.

exfoliation The process by which the outer layers of rock crumble away, leaving dome-shaped boulders or outcrops.

fertile Capable of growing and sustaining plant life or supporting farming.

fjord A coastal valley sculpted by glacial action.

floodplain A flat, low-lying area near a river or stream that is subject to flooding.

fossil The compacted and hardened remains of plants or creatures that died millions of years ago.

fossil fuels Materials that can be burned to generate energy, formed from living material that has decayed and was buried in the ground millions of years ago.

geologist A scientist who studies rocks.

glacial drift Rocks and soil carried and deposited by a glacier.

glacier A river of ice, rocks, and soil formed from densely packed snow that does not melt. Pressure forces the glacier to move slowly downhill.

gorge A deep ravine, usually with a river running through it.

groundwater An underground water source.

hydration The process by which water is absorbed into minerals in rock, expanding and weakening them.

hydraulic action When fast-flowing river water is forced into cracks in the rock along its banks, wearing it away or forcing chunks to break off.

hydrolysis The process of rocks turning into clay through chemical reactions between water and some minerals.

ice age A period in Earth's history when global temperatures dropped and ice covered large parts of the planet.

ice sheet A large, thick layer of ice covering an area of land.

igneous rock Rock formed from the cooling and hardening of hot liquid magma or lava.

inselberg A steep-sided, isolated peak made of solid rock.

karst A landscape composed of limestone features including blowholes, caves, and underground streams.

kettle lake A small lake formed when a piece of glacier ice breaks off and becomes buried. The ice eventually melts, leaving a small depression in the land that is filled with water.

landslide The rapid movement of soil and rock material down a slope.

levee A wall of sediment on either side of a river, caused by flooding.

loess A mound of fine silt deposited by the wind.

longshore drift The movement of sediment parallel to the shore when waves strike it at an angle.

magma Hot, molten rock such as that ejected from a volcano.

meander A bend in the course of a river.

meltwater A layer of water beneath a glacier, caused by great heat and pressure at its base, which makes the glacier move.

mesa A large, flat-topped but steep-sided landform.

metamorphic rock A type of rock formed when igneous, sedimentary, or other metamorphic rock is altered by intense heat and pressure.

mineral A chemical substance in Earth's crust.

mudslide The sudden movement of eroded soil mixed with water down a hill or slope.

oasis An area in a desert where the water nears the surface, forming a fertile region.

ore A mineral containing metal.

overgrazing The destruction of plant life and soil by feeding too many livestock in a particular area.

oxbow lake A lake formed by the sweeping and curving of a mature river.

oxidation The process of oxygen in the air mixing with iron in rocks to produce iron oxide, which weakens rock structure.

physical weathering When rocks are broken into smaller pieces without any change in their chemical composition.

pothole A depression in a riverbed caused by the water swirling rocks and pebbles around until they wear away the surface.

rain forest A dense forest in a hot, humid region.

rapids Fast-flowing sections of a river.

saltation The movement of sand or fine sediment by short jumps above the ground.

scree A collection of loose rocks and stones on the side of a mountain.

sediment The solid that settles at the bottom of a liquid.

sedimentary rock A type of rock formed from sediment that is compressed over time until it becomes solid.

soil erosion The process by which loose soil is washed or blown away.

soluble Capable of being dissolved.

source The place where a stream or river begins to flow.

spur A long tongue of land jutting out from the side of a valley.

surface runoff The part of rainfall that reaches streams or rivers; the remainder either evaporates into the atmosphere or seeps below ground.

tafoni A series of pits made in rock by wind and water erosion.

topsoil The fertile upper layer of soil, in which plants and crops grow best.

tributary A river or stream that flows into another body of water, such as the sea.

ventifact A loose piece of rock that has been shaped and smoothed by wind erosion.

wadi A dried-up river in a desert.

weathering The gradual breaking down of rocks and minerals into sand and soil.

yardang A streamlined hill found in desert regions, usually running in the direction of the wind.

Further Information

Books

Downs, Sandra. *Shaping the Earth: Erosion.* Brookfield, Conn.: Twenty-First Century Books, 2000.

Gifford, Clive. *The Kingfisher Geography Encyclopedia.* Boston: Kingfisher, 2003.

Luhr, James F., ed. *Earth.* New York: DK Publishing, 2003.

Pellant, Chris. *Rocks and Fossils.* Boston: Kingfisher, 2003.

Smith, Andrea Claire-Harte. *The Effects of Farming.* North Mankato, Minn.: Smart Apple Media, 2005.

Web sites

http://www.desertusa.com/
A complete guide to the rock and sand features of America's southwestern deserts.

http://www.usgs.gov/
Home page of the U.S. Geological Survey, with resources and news stories about the geography and geology of the United States.

http://members.aol.com/bowermanb/erosion.html
A valuable source containing links to more information about glaciers, soil erosion, and ocean currents.

http://www.regentsprep.org/Regents/earthsci/units/weathering/index.cfm
Learn more about weathering, erosion, and deposition on this site, which includes a glossary, reference tables, online flashcards, and quizzes.

http://volcano.und.nodak.edu/vwdocs/vwlessons/lessons/Slideshow/Slideindex.html
A guide to igneous, metamorphic, and sedimentary rocks, including photos and detailed descriptions.

Index

Acknowledgements

Picture Credits

Cover: (t) © Hans Strand/Corbis **(bl)** John Mead/Science Photo Library **(br)** © Freelance Consulting Services Pty Ltd/Corbis **6(t)** © Charles O'Rear/Corbis **6(b)** David Nunuk/Science Photo Library **7** Robert Walster/Big Blu Ltd **8** © Derek Croucher/Corbis **9(b)** Alan Sirulnikoff/Science Photo Library **10(t)** Simon Fraser/Science Photo Library **10(b)** John Mead/Science Photo Library **11(b)** Crown Copyright/Health and Safety Laboratory/ Science Photo Library **12(t)** Robert Walster/Big Blu Ltd **13** Martin Dohrn/Science Photo Library **14** © Keren Su/Corbis **15** John Mead/Science Photo Library **16(l)** Martin Bond/Science Photo Library **16(r)** Tony Craddock/Science Photo Library **17(t)** Reynolds Deon/OSF **17(b)** Martin Bond/Science Photo Library **18** © Keren Su/Corbis **19** William Ervin/Science Photo Library **20(t)** © Reuters/Corbis **20(b)** Bjorn Svensson/Science Photo Library **21** © Richard Hamilton Smith/Corbis **22(b)** CNES, 1996 Distribution Spot Image/Science Photo Library **23(t)** © Freelance Consulting Services Pty Ltd/Corbis **23(b)** NASA/Science Photo Library **26(t)** Martin Bond/ Science Photo Library **26(b)** David Nunuk/Science Photo Library **27** University of Cambridge Collection of Air Photographs/Science Photo Library **28(l)** George Post/Science Photo Library **28(r)** © George D. Lepp/Corbis **29** © Buddy Mays/Corbis **30(l)** M-Sat Ltd/Science Photo Library **31** © Hubert Stadler/Corbis **32(t)** Peter Chadwick/Science Photo Library **32(b)** Robert Walster/Big Blu Ltd **33** © Galen Rowell/Corbis **34(t)** NASA/ Science Photo Library **35** © Hans Strand/Corbis **36** © Derek Hall; Frank Lane Picture Agency/Corbis **37(t)** Steve Taylor/Science Photo Library **37(b)** © Julia Waterlow/Eye Ubiquitous/Corbis **38(t)** Novosti Press Agency/Science Photo Library **38(b)** Robert Brook/Science Photo Library **39(l)** © Michael S. Yamashita/Corbis **39(r)** © Bettmann/ Corbis **40(t)** Graham Ewens/Science Photo Library **40(b)** © David Samuel Robbins/Corbis **41** Dr Juerg Alean/Science Photo Library